Facts About the Ground Hog

By Lisa Strattin

© 2021 Lisa Strattin

FREE BOOK

FREE FOR ALL SUBSCRIBERS

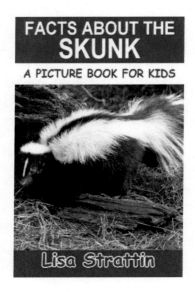

LisaStrattin.com/Subscribe-Here

BOX SET

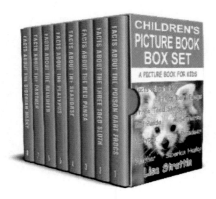

- **FACTS ABOUT THE POISON DART FROGS**
- **FACTS ABOUT THE THREE TOED SLOTH**
  - **FACTS ABOUT THE RED PANDA**
  - **FACTS ABOUT THE SEAHORSE**
  - **FACTS ABOUT THE PLATYPUS**
  - **FACTS ABOUT THE REINDEER**
  - **FACTS ABOUT THE PANTHER**
- **FACTS ABOUT THE SIBERIAN HUSKY**

LisaStrattin.com/BookBundle

Facts for Kids Picture Books by Lisa Strattin

Little Blue Penguin, Vol 92

Chipmunk, Vol 5

Frilled Lizard, Vol 39

Blue and Gold Macaw, Vol 13

Poison Dart Frogs, Vol 50

Blue Tarantula, Vol 115

African Elephants, Vol 8

Amur Leopard, Vol 89

Sabre Tooth Tiger, Vol 167

Baboon, Vol 174

Sign Up for New Release Emails Here

LisaStrattin.com/subscribe-here

Contents

INTRODUCTION

The Groundhog is a rodent that belongs to the group of marmots; they are also known as *ground squirrels.*

They are called whistlepig, groundpig and chuck. In the Northwest, they are commonly called the *Thickwood Badger.*

CHARACTERISTICS

Groundhogs are exceptionally good at burrowing and use the burrows they dig to sleep in, raise their babies and for their time of winter hibernation. Their burrows will usually have several side tunnels that lead to more rooms underground.

They will go to the trouble of digging a new *winter* burrow when they need to sleep (hibernate) through the colder months.

In some cases, they dig burrows so deep and wide that they damage the foundations of buildings in the area around their den!

APPEARANCE

Groundhogs do look very much like a fat squirrel. They have four front teeth that grow as much as 1 ½ inches per week! They constantly chew sticks and other things to wear them down, so that keeps their teeth from getting too long.

They have powerful, short legs and thick, curved claws. This helps them to be such good diggers. The groundhog's tail is only about one-fourth as long as its body.

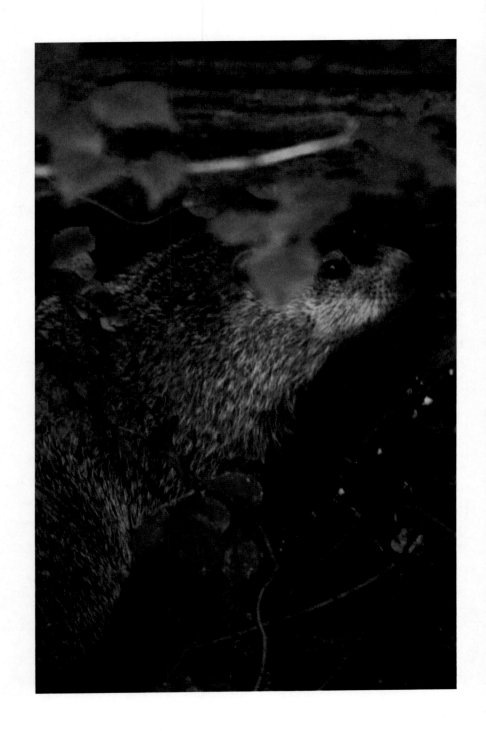

LIFE STAGES

A groundhog will usually not start a family until it is about two years old. Their breeding season is during the months of March and April, after they come out of their winter hibernation.

The female has a litter of around six babies after a month-long pregnancy and once they are born, the father leaves the burrow. The babies are born blind, helpless and without any hair, so the mother takes good care of them. Sometimes the father comes back at about the time the babies are old enough to leave the den on their own.

LIFE SPAN

A groundhog in the wild can live for as long as six years, but most only live for about three years.

In captivity, like zoos, groundhogs have been known to live for up to 14 years!

SIZE

Adult groundhogs generally grow as big as 16 inches to 2 feet in length and can weigh between 6 to just under 12 pounds. This is close to the size of many small dogs we keep as pets.

They weigh more in the winter than the spring and summer because they eat well and store fat to be able to survive through their hibernation period.

HABITAT

As we already discussed, the groundhogs live underground, in burrows they dig themselves, also called dens. This is the home they create for raising their family, sleep, and winter hibernation.

DIET

Groundhogs eat grasses, berries, and farmers' crops when they are near a farm. The really enjoy eating dandelions in the Spring when these flowers grow wild.

They also like to have occasional grasshoppers and other smaller insects, like grubs. They have been known to eat snails and other small animals.

It seems that they get the water they need from the foods they eat, rain or the morning dew right off the plants.

ENEMIES

The natural predators of the groundhogs include coyotes, bobcats, foxes, and badgers. Larger animals like the gray wolf, great horned owls, and golden eagles are known to hunt them as well.

When the groundhogs are young, they can be killed by some types of rattlesnakes, cats, and several different varieties of hawks.

Groundhogs sometimes escape a predator by climbing a tree to get away.

SUITABILITY AS PETS

Groundhogs really do belong in the wild and are not suitable as a pet. They will dig and chew through many things, and that is not good for your home!

It is best to leave them to their natural surroundings where they can live free!

COLOR ME

COLOR ME

COLOR ME

COLOR ME

COLOR ME

COLOR ME

COLOR ME

COLOR ME

COLOR ME

COLOR ME

Please leave me a review here:

LisaStrattin.com/Review-Vol-391

For more Kindle Downloads Visit Lisa Strattin Author Page on Amazon Author Central

amazon.com/author/lisastrattin

To see upcoming titles, visit my website at LisaStrattin.com– most books available on Kindle!

LisaStrattin.com

FREE BOOK

FOR ALL SUBSCRIBERS – SIGN UP NOW

Made in the USA
Las Vegas, NV
26 January 2024

84924812R00026